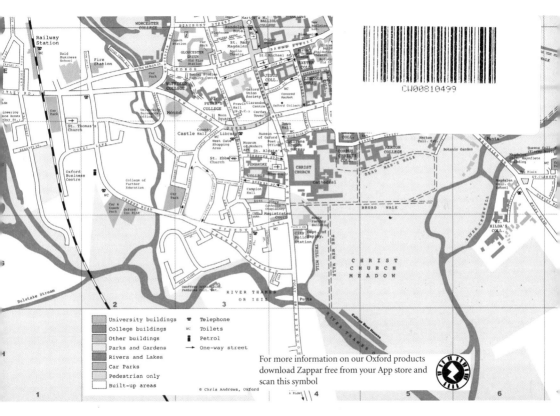

For more information on our Oxford products download Zappar free from your App store and scan this symbol

© Chris Andrews, Oxford

A LITTLE SOUVENIR
Oxford Colleges

Chris Andrews

Central Oxford and the Colleges

3

Introduction and History

Oxford has been the home of England's oldest university since before the year 1200. There were then only a few monastic schools, however in 1167 a quarrel between Henry II and Thomas Becket led to a temporary ban on English scholars going to study in France. Scholars and academics gathered in Oxford to continue with their work – fifty of them.

No-one is quite sure why Oxford was chosen as the site for England's first university – however, the town had a number of distinct advantages: Oxford was the centre of communications within its

Encaenia, the annual ceremony for giving honorary degrees.

region and both royalty and foreign scholars frequently visited the town, there were also the religious houses already established and the agricultural land was rich and fertile. Oxford was considered to be in a civilised part of England – it was near to London and getting to Europe was not necessarily a major journey. Oxford was strategically important, which had led to the building of a castle and fortifications enclosing the town (as it then was).

By 1209, it was estimated that there were 3,000 students in Oxford. It was also in 1209 that a number started to migrate to Cambridge, occurring after an unfortunate incident when some students killed a woman in Oxford. The resulting riot and

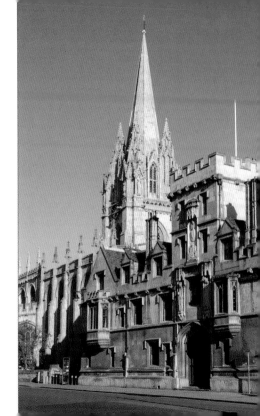

The University Church of St Mary the Virgin and All Souls College.

The High, showing Universty College, St Mary's Church and The Queen's College.

King John's permission for the execution of three of the perpetrators led to a large number of students fleeing the town, some to Cambridge and by 1284, Peterhouse College was founded.

This 13th century rioting between town and gown (townspeople and students) hastened the establishment of primitive halls of residence, at least partly as secure accommodation to protect the students. These were succeeded by the first of Oxford's colleges, which began as medieval 'halls of residence' or endowed houses under the supervision of a Master. University, Balliol and Merton Colleges, which were established between 1249 and 1266, are the oldest. The oldest endowment was Univ in 1249, however the College did not occupy its own buildings until 1331 although its statutes were approved in 1280. Balliol had its own accommodation around 1263, but no statutes until 1284, Merton had some buildings by 1266 with statutes approved by 1274. However, St Edmund Hall, the sole survivor of the medieval halls, can claim to be the oldest teaching establishment, already in existence half a century before the first three colleges. Four colleges were set up in the 14th century: Exeter, Oriel, Queen's, and New College. In the 15th century three colleges were founded by rich prelates: Lincoln, All Souls, and Magdalen. Two more colleges were founded early in the 16th century before the Reformation: Brasenose and Corpus Christi. The 16th century is remarkable for the founding of Christ Church by King Henry VIII in 1546, despite the upheaval of the Reformation. After the Reformation five colleges were set up: Trinity, St John's, and Jesus, closely followed by Wadham and Pembroke, bringing the total to fifteen. The 17th century also saw great building activity among the colleges and the emergence of two talented amateur architects: Henry Aldrich, Dean of Christ Church, and George Clarke, Fellow of All Souls, who both, with advice from the professionals such as Wren and Hawksmoor, greatly enriched Oxford architecturally.

Christ Church, Tom Tower and Quad.

University College, Radcliffe Quad.

The University also maintained its sense of importance during the 18th century and was able to add majestically to its material presence with the Clarendon Building and the Radcliffe Camera. The trustees of Dr John Radcliffe's estate also gave Oxford the Radcliffe Infirmary (1770) and the Radcliffe Observatory (1794) with its beautiful Tower of Winds. Only two colleges were founded in the 18th century – more correctly, refounded, since both had ancient antecedents and some buildings – namely Worcester and Hertford. Building work also went on at All Souls, Queen's, Magdalen, and the Radcliffe Camera.

The 19th century brought in radical reforms and far-reaching changes in university life. When college Fellows were no longer obliged to be in holy orders, were free to marry, and were required to undertake serious teaching or research, men of a different calibre were attracted to university work; the colleges began to elect Fellows for their intellectual capacity rather than for their capacity for port wine, and there were soon erudite men in the colleges. By the 1870s university life was respectable and interesting and the teaching was serious. The scene was set for the greatest revolution in the University's history: the admission of women. Between 1878 and 1898 four colleges for women and the Society of Home Students (later St Anne's) were founded; resistance to the advent of women delayed until 1920 their right to receive degrees, and the women's halls – as they technically were – did not acquire full college status until 1959.

The 19th century was remarkably expansive; besides the women's colleges, several major university buildings were put up, including the new Examination Schools in the High Street, the University Press building in Walton Street, the Ashmolean Museum in Beaumont Street, and the University Museum in Parks Road. Virtually all the existing colleges were enlarged, and Keble College was founded and built.

Fourteen new colleges were established in the 20th century; seven of these already existed in another form. The logical, even inevitable, outcome of the 19th century decision to admit women to the University has been the 20th century admission of women to the men's colleges, and then of men to the women's. One new college, Green Templeton College, was founded in 2008 following the merger of Green College and Templeton College.

There are now 38 colleges housed in buildings of richly diverse architectural styles. There are representations of the work of major architects, builders and stonemasons including Christopher Wren, Nicholas Hawksmoor, William Butterfield, William Orchard, James Stirling. The architectural and historic impact of the Oxford Colleges is known worldwide, this Little Souvenir Book will show you something of the unique attractiveness of Oxford and its atmosphere.

THE COLLEGES

All Souls College. Ninth oldest college, founded 1438 by Archbishop Chichele to pray for all the souls of the men lost in the Hundred Years War against France. Membership is for graduates only.

14 Balliol College. One of the three oldest colleges, founded by John de Balliol between 1263-84. The ancient gates (in the passage to Garden Quad above) scorched by the fire of Martyrs burned at stake outside the College in Broad Street in 1555 and 1556.

Brasenose College. Founded 1509, built on the site of Brazen Nose Hall which had a sanctuary ring or brass knocker in the shape of an animal nose on the gate, now hung in the College hall.

15

Christ Church. Founded 1525 by Cardinal Wolsey, refounded 1546 by King Henry VIII. Largest of Oxford colleges combined with the smallest cathedral in England. 13 British Prime Ministers were educated here

Christ Church Hall, Tom Tower and Cathedral
(The Hall interior is the model for Harry Potter's
Hogwarts' Hall).

Rowing at Christ Church Meadow where the River Cherwell joins the Thames (or Isis).

20   Corpus Christi College. Founded 1517, the smallest of the undergraduate colleges but not the least important. Academically eminent and also the home of the annual tortoise racing.

Exeter College. Founded 1314, the fourth oldest college. Fellows' garden (above) has good views of the Radcliffe Camera. Former members include: Burne-Jones, William Morris and JRR Tolkien.

22   Green Templeton College. Founded 2008 when Green and Templeton Colleges merged. Set up around the 18th century Radcliffe Observatory (above). Main study areas concern human welfare.

Harris Manchester College. History of independent education before becoming the second youngest of the collegiate foundations when accepted into the University in 1996. Offers a wide range of degrees for mature students (21+) only.

24 Hertford College. Founded and refounded 1740-1874. Much of the present College was build by
Thomas Jackson from 1877, including the College bridge, known as 'Oxford's Bridge of Sighs' under
which the *Encaenia* procession sometimes passes.

Jesus College. Founded 1571, has a strong Welsh connection. Small peaceful quads with flowering borders. Former members include: TE Lawrence (of Arabia), Harold Wilson. The first men's college to admit women in 1974.

Punting on the Cherwell at the Botanic Garden and Magdalen College.
Opposite: The University Cricket Pavilion and spectators in the University Parks.

Keble College. Founded 1870, known for its striking polychromatic brickwork.

Kellogg College. Founded 1990, a large international graduate college.

Lady Margaret Hall. Founded 1878 by Dame Elizabeth Wordsworth and friends to promote a university education for women. Men were admitted in 1979.

Magdalen College Tower and Christ Church field at dawn.

Linacre College. Founded 1962. A college base for visiting interdisciplinary and international graduates.

Lincoln College. Founded 1427 and 1479. Eigth oldest college. John Wesley was a fellow in the 1730s, his room inset above.

34 Magdalen College. Founded 1458, tenth oldest college. College Choir sings at dawn from the Bell Tower on May Day, to welcome spring. Past members include: Cardinal Wolsey, CS Lewis, Oscar Wilde, Dudley Moore.

Magdalen Grove with fallow deer and the New Buildings, built in 1733.

36 Mansfield College, founded 1838 and refounded in Oxford 1886. Originally a nonconformist
theological college, now open to all students.

Merton College. Founded 1264. One of the three oldest colleges, it has the largest and oldest chapel in Oxford and the College Library in Mob Quad is the oldest library in England.

Medieval books, chained to the shelves in Merton College Library situated in the 14th century Mob Quad.

New College. Founded 1379. Seventh oldest college, the Cloister (inset) is much used in filming including the Harry Potter series. Former members include: WA Spooner, creator of the 'spoonerism' also Archbishop Henry Chichele, Hugh Gaitskell, Tony Benn.

Nuffield College. Founded 1937 by William Morris (Lord Nuffield) the motor magnate to promote study of the social sciences *Opposite*: Oriel College. Founded 1326. Fifth oldest college, and the last to remain all male (until 1985).

40

Pembroke College. Founded 1624, originally to give places at Oxford to boys from Abingdon School. Past members include: Samuel Johnson, James Smithson, Roger Bannister.

The Queen's College. Founded 1341. Sixth oldest college, intended primarily for scholars from the north west of England. Front Quad built largely by Nicholas Hawksmoor, the College also has one of the largest libraries in Oxford.

Queen's College Garden, with All Souls twin towers and the Radcliffe Camera beyond

St Anne's College. Founded 1879, originally the Association for the Education of Women in Oxford, the College now accepts men and women and is one of the larger Oxford establishments.

46 St Antony's College. Founded 1950 by Antonin Besse, the only Oxford college not to be founded by a Briton. It is a world-renowned centre for research and teaching in global and regional issues.

St Catherine's College. Opened in 1962, Oxford's youngest, and largest, undergraduate and graduate college. This modernist masterpiece by the architect Arne Jacobsen is now Grade I listed.

48   St Cross College. Founded 1965, a graduate college with the main purpose to ensure that all members of the University had a college affiliation. It has a high proportion of overseas members.

St Edmund Hall was founded 1270 as an Academic Hall. It was bought in 1557 by Queen's College and achieved independent college status in 1957.

50 St Hilda's College. Founded 1893 by the Principal of Cheltenham Ladies College, to give some of her students a place at Oxford. Now welcomes all applicants to the lovely riverside setting.

St Hugh's College. Founded 1886, a second foundation by Dame Elizabeth Wordsworth. Now one of the larger Oxford colleges with around 800 students, the gardens and grounds are particularly fine.

52 St John's College. Founded 1555 by Thomas White, a Roman Catholic in the year the Protestant Bishops were martyred. Most famous member was William Laud, scholar, Fellow and President of the College. He was Chancellor of the University 1629-40 and Archbishop of Canterbury in 1633.

Decorative rainwater goods and stone carvings in St John's Canterbury Quad.

54 St Peter's College. Founded 1929, originally with only 40 students. The newest college to be founded within the old city wall and the buildings are a mix of Georgian and bold modern architecture.

Somerville College. Founded 1879. Though the College was originally all women, in 1994 it accepted men. Many great scientists, novelists and politicians have studied here including Vera Brittain, Dorothy L Sayers, Dorothy Hodgkin, Indira Gandhi and Margaret Thatcher.

56 Trinity College. Founded 1555 as a training house for Catholic priests. The site of the college, now very much in the city centre, was originally chosen for its quiet, rural aspect.

Trinity's Garden Quad, the original part of which was designed by Christopher Wren, is often used to host events including the College barbecue and summer plays.

58 University College. Founded 1249. The oldest collegiate foundation. The poet Shelley was briefly an undergraduate and his memorial (inset) is here. Past members include: Dr John Radcliffe, CS Lewis and Bill Clinton.

Wadham College. Founded 1610. The buildings are some of the most harmonious in Oxford, and were built in under three years by Dorothy, widow of the founder Nicholas Wadham. John Wilkins (Warden) and Christopher Wren were members and founded The Royal Society in London in 1660.

Wolfson College. Founded 1965 to provide a college life for graduates that were otherwise unattached to a specific college. The modern riverside buildings sit in nearly thirteen acres of gardens.

Worcester College. Founded 1714, however Gloucester College was founded on this site in 1283 by the Benedictine Abbey of St Peter at Gloucester as a place of study. It is the only Oxford college to have its own lake.

The Oxford Spires